Prayers of the Advent and Christmas Seasons

D1455709

Bishops' Committee on the Liturgy
National Conference of Catholic Bishops
United States Catholic Conference
Washington, D.C.

BV
40
.P73
1989

In its planning document, as approved by the general membership of
the National Conference of Catholic Bishops in November 1987, the
Bishops' Committee on the Liturgy was authorized to prepare a book of
prayers and blessings for use by Catholic families and households.
Prayers of the Advent and Christmas Seasons is excerpted from that book
Catholic Household Blessings and Prayers, which was approved by the
NCCB Administrative Committee in March 1988, and is authorized for
publication by the undersigned.

Reverend Robert N. Lynch
General Secretary
July 10, 1989   NCCB/USCC

ISBN 1-55586-300-0

Contents

Contents

FOREWORD

The heart of renewal is prayer. And the key to renewing prayer is enkindling a love and practice of prayer in the hearts of those who make up the Church. Roman Catholics, like any people who share a faith and a way of life, need the words and gestures that express that faith and teach that way of life.

This book of prayers is offered so that all Catholics may have access to their heritage and may come to know the prayers that are both their duty and their privilege. It is meant to be a way of reminding and a way of learning what belongs to us. For all who make up the Church, these prayers and rites are something that we take with reverence for all the generations that have shaped them for us. We will give something of ourselves to these prayers, something that they yet lack, something that can form Christians in our time and place. Then we will hand them on, for they are not finally ours. They belong to the communion of saints in which we walk and in which our children walk and their children may also walk.

Finally, whether we say, "God bless you," or join in a rite of song and prayer and Scripture, we are proclaiming the good news of God's love and reign.

ADVENT AND CHRISTMAS

INTRODUCTION

Advent is a time of waiting, listening, holding back, and discovering the beauty in both the night and the day. Christmas is a festival that has many days: the Nativity itself; Saint Stephen; Saint John; Holy Innocents; Holy Family; Mary, Mother of God; Epiphany; and the Baptism of the Lord. The Christmas spirit springs from the delight and the terror of birth itself: the Word made flesh, the very presence of God with us. The "wonderful exchange," God sharing our human condition, and we caught up into God's grace, is the Church's reflection and song all through Advent and Christmas.

Year by year, we learn what it is to keep Advent: to take time with those days and nights before Christmas. And we learn too to keep Christmas: to make a festival of stories, songs, and deeds done year after year. Together the keeping of these seasons gives witness to how God reigns in our lives and in the world. Throughout these days of Advent and Christmas, the images of the nativity and of the final coming of our Messiah are placed side by side with the gospel we have believed: God-within us, now, in our brothers and sisters.

Table prayers for Advent and Christmas are found on pages 26 and 32. The following blessings may be used at moments when the household has come together. The Sunday after Christmas is the feast of the Holy Family. On that day, the blessing of a family on page 37 is appropriate.

BLESSING OF AN ADVENT WREATH

The Advent wreath is made of four candles and a circle of branches. Before the first candle is lighted, the household gathers for this blessing.

All make the sign of the cross. The leader begins:

Our help is in the name of the Lord.

All respond:

Who made heaven and earth.

The leader may use these or similar words to introduce the blessing:

In the short days and long nights of Advent, we realize how we are always waiting for deliverance, always needing salvation by our God. Around this wreath, we shall remember God's promise.

Then the Scripture is read:

Listen to the words of the prophet Isaiah:

The people who walked in darkness
   have seen a great light;
Upon those who dwelt in the land of gloom
   a light has shone.
You have brought them abundant joy
   and great rejoicing.

Isaiah 9:1-2

(The family's Bible may be used for an alternate reading, such as Isaiah 63:16-17 or Isaiah 64:2-7.)

The reader concludes:

This is the Word of the Lord.

All respond:

Thanks be to God.

After a time of silence, all join in prayers of intercession and in the Lord's Prayer.

Then the leader invites:

Let us now pray for God's blessing upon us and upon this wreath.

After a short silence, the leader prays:

Lord our God,
we praise you for your Son, Jesus Christ:
he is Emmanuel, the hope of the peoples,
he is the wisdom that teaches and guides us,
he is the Savior of every nation.

Lord God,
let your blessing come upon us
as we light the candles of this wreath.
May the wreath and its light
be a sign of Christ's promise to bring us
  salvation.
May he come quickly and not delay.

We ask this through Christ our Lord.
R. Amen.

The first candle is then lighted.

The leader says:

Let us bless the Lord.

All respond, making the sign of the cross:

Thanks be to God.

*The blessing concludes with a verse from
"O Come, O Come, Emmanuel":*

O come, desire of nations, bind
In one the hearts of humankind;
Bid ev'ry sad divisions cease
And by thyself our Prince of peace.
Rejoice! Rejoice! Emmanuel
Shall come to thee, O Israel.

*Each day in Advent, perhaps at the evening meal
(see prayer on page 26), the candles are lighted:
one candle the first week, two the second, and so
forth.*

BLESSING OF A CHRISTMAS TREE

When the tree has been prepared, the household gathers around it. All make the sign of the cross.

The leader begins:

Blessed be the name of the Lord.

All respond:

Now and for ever.

The leader may use these or similar words to introduce the blessing:

This tree is a blessing to our home. It reminds us of all that is beautiful, all that is filled with the gentleness and the promise of God. It stands in our midst as a tree of light that we might promise such beauty to one another and to our world. It stands like that tree of paradise that God made into the tree of life, the cross of Jesus.

Then the Scripture is read:

Listen to the words of the apostle Paul to Titus:

But when the kindness and generous love of
    God our savior appeared,
not because of any righteous deeds we had done
    but because of his mercy,

he saved us through the bath of rebirth
    and renewal by the holy Spirit,
whom he richly poured out on us
    through Jesus Christ our savior,
so that we might be justified by his grace
    and become heirs in hope of eternal life.

Titus 3:4-7

*(The family's Bible may be used for an alternate
reading such as Psalm 96:11-13.)*

The reader concludes:

This is the Word of the Lord.

All respond:

Thanks be to God.

*After a time of silence, all join in prayers of
intercession and in the Lord's Prayer. Then the
leader invites:*

Let us now pray for God's blessing upon all who
gather around this tree.

After a short silence, the leader prays:

A Lord our God,
    we praise you for the light of creation:
    the sun, the moon, and the stars of the night.
    We praise you for the light of Israel:
    the Law, the prophets, and the wisdom of
        the Scriptures.

We praise you for Jesus Christ, your Son:
he is Emmanuel, God-with-us, the Prince of
    Peace,
who fills us with the wonder of your love.

Lord God,
let your blessing come upon us
as we illumine this tree.
May the light and cheer it gives
be a sign of the joy that fills our hearts.
May all who delight in this tree
come to the knowledge and joy of salvation.

We ask this through Christ our Lord.
R. Amen.

Or:

B God of all creation,
we praise you for this tree
which brings beauty and memories and the
    promise of life to our home.
May your blessing be upon all who gather
    around this tree,
all who keep the Christmas festival by its
    lights.
We wait for the coming of the Christ,
the days of everlasting justice and of peace.
You are our God, living and reigning, for ever
    and ever.
R. Amen.

The lights of the tree are then illuminated.

The leader says:

Let us bless the Lord.

All respond, making the sign of the cross:

Thanks be to God.

The blessing concludes with a verse from "O Come, O Come, Emmanuel":

O come, thou dayspring, come and cheer
Our spirits by thine advent here;
Disperse the gloomy clouds of night
And death's dark shadow put to flight.
Rejoice! Rejoice! Emmanuel
Shall come to thee, O Israel.

BLESSING OF A CHRISTMAS CRÈCHE OR MANGER SCENE

The manger scene has a special place near the Christmas tree or in another place where family members can reflect and pray during the Christmas season. It is blessed each year on Christmas Eve or Christmas Day.

All make the sign of the cross. The leader begins:

Our help is in the name of the Lord.

All respond:

Who made heaven and earth.

The leader may use these or similar words to introduce the blessing:

We are at the beginning of the days of Christmas. All through the season we will look on these images of sheep and cattle, of shepherds, of Mary and of Joseph and Jesus.

Then the Scripture is read:

Listen to the words of the holy gospel according to Luke:

In those days a decree went out from Caesar Augustus that the whole world should be enrolled. This was the first enrollment, when Quirinius was governor of Syria. So all went to be enrolled, each to his own town. And Joseph too went up from Galilee from the town of Nazareth to Judea, to the city of David that is called Bethlehem, because he was of the house and family of David, to be enrolled with Mary, his betrothed, who was with child. While they were there, the time came for her to have her child, and she gave birth to her firstborn son. She wrapped him in swaddling clothes and laid him in a manger, because there was no room for them in the inn.

Luke 2:1-7

The reader concludes:

This is the Gospel of the Lord.

All respond:

Praise to you, Lord Jesus Christ.

The figures may be placed in the manger. After a time of silence, all join in prayers of intercession and in the Lord's Prayer.

Then the leader invites:

Pray now for God's blessing as we look on these figures.

After a short silence, the leader prays:

A God of every nation and people,
   from the very beginning of creation
   you have made manifest your love:
   when our need for a Savior was great
   you sent your Son to be born of the
      Virgin Mary.
   To our lives he brings joy and peace,
   justice, mercy, and love.

Lord,
bless all who look upon this manger;
may it remind us of the humble birth of Jesus,
and raise our thoughts to him,
who is God-with-us and Savior of all,
and who lives and reigns for ever and ever.
R. Amen.

Or:

B God of Mary and Joseph, of shepherds and
      animals,
   bless us whenever we gaze on this manger
      scene.
   Through all the days of Christmas
   may these figures tell the story
   of how humans, angels, and animals
   found the Christ in this poor place.

Fill our house with hospitality, joy,
gentleness, and thanksgiving
and guide our steps in the way of peace.

Grant this through Christ our Lord.
R. Amen.

The leader says:

Let us bless the Lord.

All respond, making the sign of the cross:

Thanks be to God.

*Then Christmas songs and carols are sung,
for example:*

It came upon the midnight clear,
That glorious song of old,
From angels bending near the earth
To touch their harps of gold:
"Peace on the earth, good will to all
From heaven's all gracious King";
The world in solemn stillness lay,
To hear the angels sing.

Yet with the woes of sin and strife,
The world has suffered long;
Beneath the heav'nly hymn have rolled
Two thousand years of wrong;
And warring humankind hears not
The tidings which they bring;
O hush the noise and cease your strife
And hear the angels sing.

Edmond Sears (alt.)

15

BLESSING FOR THE NEW YEAR

On New Year's Eve or New Year's Day, the household gathers at the table or at the Christmas tree or manger scene. Many people make New Year's Day a day of prayer for peace. The calendar of the new year may be held during the blessing.

All make the sign of the cross. The leader begins:

Let us praise the Lord of days and seasons and
   years, saying: Glory to God in the highest!

All respond:

And peace to his people on earth!

*The leader may use these or similar words to
introduce the blessing:*

Our lives are made of days and nights, of seasons and years, for we are part of a universe of suns and moons and planets. We mark ends and we make beginnings and, in all, we praise God for the grace and mercy that fill our days.

Then the Scripture is read:

Listen to the words of the book of Genesis:

God said: "Let there be lights in the dome of the
sky, to separate day from night. Let them mark
the fixed times, the days and the years, and serve
as luminaries in the dome of the sky, to shed
light upon the earth." And so it happened: God
made the two great lights, the greater one to
govern the day, and the lesser one to govern the
night; and he made the stars. God set them in
the dome of the sky, to shed light upon the
earth, to govern the day and the night, and to
separate the light from the darkness. God saw
how good it was. Evening came, and morning
followed—the fourth day.

Genesis 1:14-19

*(The family's Bible may be used for an alternate
reading such as Psalm 90:1-4.)*

The reader concludes:

This is the Word of the Lord.

All respond:

Thanks be to God.

17

After a time of silence, members of the household offer prayers of thanksgiving for the past year, and of intercession for the year to come. On January 1, it may be appropriate to conclude these prayers with the Litany of Loreto (page 43) since this is the solemn feast of Mary, Mother of God. In conclusion, all join hands for the Lord's Prayer.

Then the leader begins:

Let us now pray for God's blessing in the new year.

After a short silence, parents may place their hands on their children in blessing as the leader says:

Remember us, O God;
from age to age be our comforter.
You have given us the wonder of time,
blessings in days and nights, seasons and years.

Bless your children at the turning of the year
and fill the months ahead with the bright hope
that is ours in the coming of Christ.

You are our God, living and reigning, for ever
and ever.
R. Amen.

Another prayer for peace may be said:

Lord, make me an instrument of your peace:
where there is hatred, let me sow love;
where there is injury, pardon;
where there is doubt, faith;
where there is despair, hope;
where there is darkness, light;
where there is sadness, joy.

O divine Master, grant that I may not so much
    seek
to be consoled as to console,
to be understood as to understand,
to be loved as to love.
For it is in giving that we receive,
it is in pardoning that we are pardoned,
it is in dying that we are born to eternal life.
R. Amen.

St. Francis of Assisi

The leader says:

Let us bless the Lord.

All respond, making the sign of the cross:

Thanks be to God.

*Then the following verse may be sung to a tune
such as "The Old Hundreth" (Praise God from
Whom All Blessings Flow). It may be appropriate
to exchange a greeting of peace or to join in toasts
for the old and new year.*

Great God, we sing that mighty hand
By which supported still we stand;
The opening year your mercy showed;
That mercy crowns it till it close.

BLESSING OF THE HOME AND HOUSEHOLD ON THE EPIPHANY

The traditional date of Epiphany is January 6, but in the United States it is celebrated on the Sunday between January 2 and January 8. Some communities have the custom of blessing homes while recalling the visit of the Magi. The household gathers at the manger scene.

All make the sign of the cross. The leader begins:

Peace be with this house and with all who live here. Blessed be the name of the Lord.

All respond:

Now and for ever.

The leader may use these or similar words to introduce the blessing:

During these days of the Christmas season, we keep this feast of Epiphany, celebrating the manifestation of Christ to the Magi, to John in the River Jordan, and to the disciples at the wedding at Cana. Today Christ is manifest to us! Today this home is a holy place.

Then the Scripture is read:

Listen to the words of the holy gospel according to John:

In the beginning was the Word,
  and the Word was with God,
  and the Word was God.
He was in the beginning with God.
All things came to be through him,
  and without him nothing came to be.

And the Word became flesh
  and made his dwelling among us,
  and we saw his glory,
  the glory as of the Father's only Son,
  full of grace and truth.

John 1:1-3,14

(The family's Bible may be used for an alternate reading such as Matthew 2:1-12.)

The reader concludes:

This is the Gospel of the Lord.

All respond:

Praise to you, Lord Jesus Christ.

Everyone then processes from one room to another. In each room, God's blessing is asked on all that takes place in that room. Blessed water may be carried and sprinkled. When all return to the starting place, they join in the Lord's Prayer.

Then the leader begins:

Let us pray.

After a short silence, the leader continues:

A Lord God of heaven and earth,
you revealed your only-begotten Son to every
    nation
by the guidance of a star.

Bless this house
and all who inhabit it.

Fill them (us) with the light of Christ,
that their (our) concern for others may reflect
    your love.

We ask this through Christ our Lord.
R. Amen.

Or:

B Lord our God, bless this household.
May we be blessed with health, goodness of
    heart,
gentleness, and the keeping of your law.
We give thanks to you,
Father, Son, and Holy Spirit,
now and for ever.
R. Amen.

The leader says:

Let us bless the Lord.

All respond, making the sign of the cross:

Thanks be to God.

The blessing concludes with an appropriate song, for example, "O Come, All Ye Faithful" or "We Three Kings."

APPENDIX

AT TABLE DURING ADVENT

*Advent candles may be lighted
as the leader says:*

Blessed are you, Lord, God
 of all creation:
in the darkness and in the light.

Blessed are you
in this food and in our sharing.

Blessed are you as we wait
 in joyful hope
for the coming of our savior,
 Jesus Christ.

All respond:

For the kingdom, the power, and the
glory are yours, now and for ever.

The leader says:

Come, Lord Jesus!

All respond:

Come quickly!

Another form of Advent prayer begins with the sign of the cross.

In the name of the Father, and of the Son, and of the Holy Spirit. Amen.

Someone at table reads one of the following Scriptures or the Scripture assigned to the liturgy of the day.

A Listen to the words of the prophet Isaiah:

Trust in the LORD forever!
  For the LORD is an eternal Rock.
He humbles those in high places,
  and the lofty city he brings down;
He tumbles it to the ground,
  levels it with the dust.
It is trampled underfoot by the needy,
  by the footsteps of the poor.

Isaiah 26:4-6

Or:

B Listen to the words of the prophet
Isaiah:

I am the LORD and there is no other,
there is no God besides me.

I form the light, and create the
darkness,
I make well-being and create woe;
I, the Lord, do all these things.
Let justice descend, O heavens, like dew
from above,
like gentle rain let the skies drop it
down.
Let the earth open and salvation bud
forth;
let justice also spring up!
I, the LORD, have created this.

Isaiah 45:5a,7-8

The reader concludes:

This is the Word of the Lord.

All respond:

Thanks be to God.

The leader invites:

Lift up your hearts.

All respond:

We lift them up to the Lord.

Then the leader prays:

God, the Father of mercies,
you willed your Son to take flesh,
in order to give life back to us.
Bless these your gifts
with which we are about to nourish our
    bodies,
so that, receiving new strength, we may
    wait in watchfulness
for the glorious coming of Christ.

We ask this through the same Christ our
    Lord.
R. Amen.

AFTER THE MEAL

The leader says:

Let us live soberly, justly, and devoutly in
    this world
as we wait in joyful hope
for the coming of our Savior, Jesus Christ.

All respond:

For the kingdom, the power, and the
glory are yours, now and for ever.

See also the Advent Wreath blessing on page 5.
On the last days before Christmas, the following
prayers are added:

December 17:
O Wisdom, O holy Word of God,
you govern all creation with
    your strong yet tender care.
Come and show your people the way to
    salvation.

December 18:
O sacred Lord of ancient Israel,
who showed yourself to Moses in the burning
    bush,
who gave him the holy law on Sinai mountain:
come, stretch out your mighty hand to set us
    free.

December 19:
O Flower of Jesse's stem,
you have been raised up as a sign for all peoples;
kings stand silent in your presence;
the nations bow down in worship before you.
Come, let nothing keep you from coming to our
    aid.

December 20:
O Key of David, O royal Power of Israel
    controlling at your will the gate of heaven:
come, break down the prison walls of death
    for those who dwell in darkness and the
        shadow of death;
and lead your captive people into freedom.

December 21:
O Radiant Dawn, splendor of eternal light,
  sun of justice:
come, shine on those who dwell in darkness
  and the shadow of death.

December 22:
O King of all the nations,
the only joy of every human heart;
O Keystone of the mighty arch of humankind,
come and save the creature you fashioned from
  the dust.

December 23:
O Emmanuel, king and lawgiver,
desire of the nations,
Savior of all people,
come and set us free, Lord our God.

AT TABLE DURING CHRISTMASTIME

A Christmas candle may be lighted as the leader says:

Glory to God in the highest.

All respond:

And peace to his people on earth.

The leader prays:

Lord Jesus,
in the peace of this season
our spirits rejoice:
With the beasts and angels,
the shepherds and stars,
with Mary and Joseph
we sing God's praise.

By your coming
may the hungry be filled with
    good things,
and may our table and home be
    blessed.

Glory to God in the highest.

All respond:

And peace to his people on earth.

Another form of Christmas prayer begins with the sign of the cross.

In the name of the Father, and of the Son, and of the Holy Spirit. Amen.

Someone at table reads one of the following Scriptures or the text assigned to the liturgy of the day.

A Listen to the words of the holy gospel according to John:

And the Word became flesh
and made his dwelling among us,
and we saw his glory,

the glory as of the Father's only Son,
full of grace and truth.

John 1:14

Or:

B Listen to the words of the prophet
Isaiah:

I rejoice heartily in the LORD,
 in my God is the joy of my soul;
For he has clothed me with a robe of
 salvation,
 and wrapped me in a mantle of justice,
Like a bridegroom adorned with a
 diadem,
 like a bride bedecked with her jewels.
As the earth brings forth its plants,
 and a garden makes its growth spring
 up,
So will the LORD GOD make justice and
 praise
 spring up before all the nations.

Isaiah 61:10-11

The reader concludes:

This is the Word of the Lord.

All respond:

Thanks be to God.

The leader invites:

Lift up your hearts.

All respond:

We lift them up to the Lord.

Then the leader prays:

Blessed are you, Lord God.
Through the fruitful virginity of Mary
you fulfilled the long expectation
    of the poor and oppressed.
Grant that with the same faith
    with which Mary awaited the birth of
        her Son,
we may look for him in our brothers and
    sisters in need.

We ask this through Christ our Lord.
R. Amen.

AFTER THE MEAL

The leader says:

The Word became flesh, alleluia.

All respond:

And dwelt among us, alleluia.

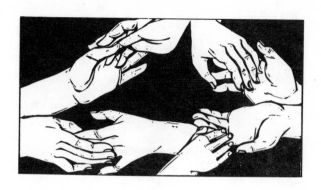

BLESSING FOR
A FAMILY OR HOUSEHOLD

This rite may be used annually on a day of special significance to a family, or at times when members of the family who live far apart have come together, or at times when the family experiences special difficulties or special joys. The leader may be someone from outside the family (a priest, deacon, or lay minister) or may be one of the family members. The blessing may be given at a family meal or another appropriate time.

All make the sign of the cross. The leader begins:

The grace of our Lord Jesus Christ be with us all, now and for ever.
R. Amen.

The leader may use these words or words directed to the specific occasion to introduce the blessing:

We are a family. For one another, we are love and trial, strength and trouble. Even when far apart, we belong to one another and, in various ways, we remember and pray for one another. We join now to give thanks to our God and to ask God's blessing on this family (those who are present and those who are not here).

Then the Scripture is read:

Listen to the words of the apostle Paul to the Colossians:

Put on then, as God's chosen ones, holy and beloved, heartfelt compassion, kindness, humility, gentleness, and patience, bearing with one another and forgiving one another, if one has a grievance against another; as the Lord has forgiven you, so must you also do. And over all these put on love, that is, the bond of perfection. And let the peace of Christ control your hearts, the peace into which you were also called in one body. And be thankful. Let the word of Christ dwell in you richly, as in all wisdom you teach and admonish one another, singing psalms, hymns, and spiritual songs with gratitude in your hearts to God. And whatever you do, in word or

in deed, do everything in the name of the Lord
Jesus, giving thanks to God the Father through
him.

Colossians 3:12-17

*(The family's Bible may be used for an alternate
reading such as Ephesians 4:1-6 or 1 Corinthians
12:31—13:7.)*

The reader concludes:

This is the Word of the Lord.

All respond:

Thanks be to God.

*After a time of silence, all offer prayers of
intercession, remembering especially those who
have died. Then all join hands for the Lord's
Prayer.*

The leader says the prayer of blessing:

A   O God,
   you have created us in love and saved us in
      mercy,
   and through the bond of marriage
   you have established the family
   and willed that it should become a sign
      of Christ's love for his Church.

   Shower your blessings on this family
      gathered here in your name.

Enable those who are joined by one love
to support one another
by their fervor of spirit and devotion to
    prayer.
Make them responsive to the needs of others
and witnesses to the faith in all they say and
    do.

We ask this through Christ our Lord.
R. Amen.

Or:

B In good times and in bad,
in sickness and in health,
we belong to each other
as we belong to you, God ever faithful.
By morning and by night
may your name be on our lips,
a blessing to all our days:
so may kindness and patience be ever among
    us,
a hunger for justice,
and songs of thankfulness in all we do.

We ask this through Christ our Lord.
R. Amen.

*The leader may sprinkle all with holy water, or
each one may take holy water and make the sign of
the cross.*

The leader concludes:

May the Lord Jesus,
who lived with his holy family in Nazareth,
dwell also with your (our) family,
keep it from all evil,
and make all of you (us) one in heart and mind.
R. Amen.

The leader says:

Let us bless the Lord.

All respond, making the sign of the cross:

Thanks be to God.

The blessing may conclude with singing "Now Thank We All Our God," (page 42) or another appropriate song.

NOW THANK WE ALL OUR GOD

Now thank we all our God with hearts and
  hands and voices,
Who wondrous things has done, in whom this
  world rejoices;
Who, from our mothers' arms, has blessed us on
  our way
With countless gifts of love, and still in ours
  today.

O may this gracious God through all our life be
  near us,
With ever joyful hearts and blessed peace to
  cheer us;
Preserve us in this grace, and guide us in
  distress,
And free us from all sin, till heaven we possess.

Martin Rinkart

LITANY OF LORETO

Lord, have mercy	Lord, have mercy
Christ, have mercy	Christ, have mercy
Lord, have mercy	Lord, have mercy

God our Father in heaven	have mercy on us
God the Son, Redeemer of the world	have mercy on us
God the Holy Spirit	have mercy on us
Holy Trinity, one God	have mercy on us

Holy Mary	pray for us
Holy Mother of God	pray for us
Most honored of virgins	pray for us

Mother of Christ	pray for us
Mother of the Church	pray for us
Mother of divine grace	pray for us
Mother most pure	pray for us
Mother of chaste love	pray for us
Mother and virgin	pray for us
Sinless Mother	pray for us

Dearest of mothers	pray for us
Model of motherhood	pray for us
Mother of good counsel	pray for us
Mother of our Creator	pray for us
Mother of our Savior	pray for us
Virgin most wise	pray for us
Virgin rightly praised	pray for us
Virgin rightly renowned	pray for us
Virgin most powerful	pray for us
Virgin gentle in mercy	pray for us
Faithful Virgin	pray for us
Mirror of justice	pray for us
Throne of wisdom	pray for us
Cause of our joy	pray for us
Shrine of the Spirit	pray for us
Glory of Israel	pray for us
Vessel of selfless devotion	pray for us
Mystical Rose	pray for us
Tower of David	pray for us
Tower of ivory	pray for us
House of gold	pray for us
Ark of the covenant	pray for us
Gate of heaven	pray for us
Morning Star	pray for us
Health of the sick	pray for us
Refuge of sinners	pray for us
Comfort of the troubled	pray for us
Help of Christians	pray for us
Queen of angels	pray for us
Queen of patriarchs and prophets	pray for us

Queen of apostles and martyrs	pray for us
Queen of confessors and virgins	pray for us
Queen of all saints	pray for us
Queen conceived without sin	pray for us
Queen assumed into heaven	pray for us
Queen of the rosary	pray for us
Queen of peace	pray for us
Lamb of God, you take away the sins of the world	have mercy on us
Lamb of God, you take away the sins of the world	have mercy on us
Lamb of God, you take away the sins of the world	have mercy on us

V. Pray for us, holy Mother of God.
R. That we may become worthy of the promises of Christ.

Let us pray.

Eternal God,
let your people enjoy constant health in mind and body.
Through the intercession of the Virgin Mary
free us from the sorrows of this life
and lead us to happiness in the life to come.
Grant this through Christ our Lord.
R. Amen.

DATE DUE

NOV 2 ʀ '90		
DEC 1 7 '90		
JAN 1 3 1993		